CHRISTINE HAGGINS

Prayers for Good Health

Spiritual Guidance for Healing, Strength, and Wholeness

First edition

This book was professionally typeset on Reedsy.
Find out more at reedsy.com

Contents

THE GIFT OF HEALTH

The Importance of Prayer in Health

Health is one of the most precious gifts we can receive, yet it's something we often take for granted until it's compromised. The journey toward good health encompasses not just the physical body but also the mind and spirit. It's a holistic experience that involves nurturing every aspect of our being. In today's fast-paced world, it's easy to become overwhelmed by stress, worry, and the challenges of daily life. These pressures can take a toll on our health, leading to physical ailments, emotional unrest, and spiritual weariness.

This is where prayer comes in as a powerful and transformative practice. Prayer is more than just a religious obligation or a ritual; it is a profound means of communication with the Divine. Through prayer, we can seek comfort, guidance, and strength in times of need. When it comes to health, prayer serves as a bridge that connects our deepest desires for well-being with the Divine source of all healing and wholeness.

Throughout history, people of all faiths have turned to prayer during times of illness and health challenges. It's a practice that transcends cultures and religions, embodying a universal longing for healing and protection. Prayer has the power to calm the mind, soothe the spirit, and even influence physical healing. Studies have shown that individuals who engage in regular prayer and meditation experience reduced stress, better mental health, and improved overall well-being.

The act of praying for health allows us to surrender our worries and fears, placing our trust in a higher power. It encourages a mindset of hope, positivity, and resilience. Prayer for health is not only about asking for physical healing but also about seeking peace, acceptance, and the strength to face whatever challenges may come. It's about acknowledging that we are not alone in our struggles and that there is a source of infinite love and power that we can draw upon.

In this prayer book, you will find prayers specifically designed to address various aspects of health. These prayers are not just words to be recited; they are a means of opening your heart and mind to the healing power of the Divine. Whether you are seeking physical healing, emotional balance, or spiritual renewal, these prayers are here to guide you on your journey toward good health. They are tools to help you connect with God, to express your deepest needs and desires, and to find the strength to persevere.

How to Use This Prayer Book

This prayer book is intended to be a companion on your journey to good health. It is structured in a way that allows you to easily find the prayers that resonate most with your current needs. Whether you are dealing with a specific health issue, seeking general wellness, or praying for the health of a loved one, you will find prayers that speak to your situation.

Here are some suggestions on how to make the most of this prayer book:

Start with the Introduction and Purpose

Before diving into the specific prayers, take some time to read through the introduction and understand the purpose of this book. Reflect on your own health journey and what you hope to gain from this prayer practice. Setting an intention before you begin can help you focus your prayers and open your heart to the healing process.

Use the Table of Contents to Navigate

The book is organized into thematic sections, each focusing on different aspects of health. Use the Table of Contents to navigate to the sections that are most relevant to you. Whether you need a prayer for physical healing, emotional support, or spiritual strength, you can quickly find what you are looking for.

Take Time to Reflect

Each prayer is designed to be more than just a recitation of words. Take time to reflect on the meaning of the prayers and how they apply to your life. You might want to read a prayer several times, meditate on the words, and let them sink into your heart. You can also journal your thoughts and feelings after praying, using the Personal Prayer Journal section at the end of the book.

Integrate Prayer into Your Daily Routine

To fully benefit from this prayer book, try to integrate prayer into your daily routine. You can start your day with a prayer for strength and energy, or end your day with a prayer of gratitude for your health. You can also use these prayers during moments of quiet reflection, meditation, or whenever you feel the need for spiritual support.

Customize the Prayers to Fit Your Needs

The prayers in this book are meant to be a guide, but feel free to customize them to fit your specific needs. You can add your own words, focus on particular aspects of your health, or adapt the prayers to your personal beliefs. The most important thing is that the prayers resonate with you and help you feel connected to the Divine.

Share the Prayers with Others

If you know someone who is struggling with health issues, consider sharing a prayer from this book with them. Praying for others is a powerful way to offer support and compassion. You can also pray together, creating a sense of community and shared spiritual strength.

Understanding the Holistic Nature of Health

Health is not just the absence of illness; it is a state of complete physical, emotional, and spiritual well-being. To achieve good health, we must take care of every aspect of our being. This prayer book recognizes the holistic nature of health and offers prayers that address all dimensions of well-being.

Physical Health

Our bodies are temples, and maintaining physical health is essential for living a full and vibrant life. The prayers in this book for physical health focus on healing from illness, protecting against disease, and maintaining strength and vitality. Whether you are recovering from a sickness, seeking relief from chronic pain, or simply wanting to improve your overall health, these prayers will guide you in asking for Divine intervention and support.

Emotional Health

Emotional health is just as important as physical health. Our emotions affect how we perceive the world, interact with others, and cope with life's challenges. This book includes prayers that focus on emotional balance, mental clarity, and overcoming anxiety and depression. By praying for emotional health, you invite peace, joy, and resilience into your life, enabling you to handle stress and adversity with grace.

Spiritual Health

At the core of our being is our spirit, the source of our deepest beliefs, values, and sense of purpose. Spiritual health is about nurturing this inner self, maintaining a strong connection with God, and finding meaning in life. The prayers for spiritual health in this book are designed to renew your faith, deepen your spiritual practice, and bring you closer to the Divine. They encourage you to seek not only physical and emotional healing but also spiritual growth and fulfillment.

Embracing the Journey

The journey to good health is a lifelong process. It's about making daily choices that support your well-being, cultivating habits that nourish your body, mind, and spirit, and turning to prayer as a source of strength and guidance. This prayer book is here to support you on that journey, offering prayers that you can return to again and again.

Remember, good health is a gift that must be cherished and nurtured. Through prayer, you can connect with the Divine source of all health and healing, finding the strength, peace, and resilience you need to live a healthy, fulfilling life.

As you begin this journey, may you be blessed with good health, a peaceful mind, and a joyful spirit. May the prayers in this book be a source of comfort and strength, guiding you toward the wholeness and well-being that you seek.

PRAYERS FOR PHYSICAL HEALTH

Prayer for Healing from Illness

Illness can be a difficult and trying experience, affecting not only the body but also the mind and spirit. When we are faced with sickness, it's natural to feel vulnerable, frightened, and even hopeless at times. However, illness is also a moment when we can turn to prayer as a source of comfort and strength, trusting in God's power to heal and restore us.

Dear Lord,

I come before You today with a heart burdened by illness. My body is weak, and my spirit is weary. I ask for Your healing touch to restore me to health. I know that You are the Great Physician, and there is no ailment too great for You to heal. Please ease my pain, comfort my soul, and bring relief to my body. Grant me patience and strength as I go through this time of healing, and help me to trust in Your perfect plan for my life.

Amen.

This prayer invites the Divine into the healing process, acknowledging that God's power transcends human understanding. It's important to recognize that healing may not always come in the way we expect. Sometimes, it's a gradual process, and other times, it might mean finding peace in the midst of suffering. Regardless of the outcome, this prayer is a reminder to place our trust in God's wisdom and care.

In addition to praying for healing, consider incorporating scripture into your prayers. For instance, **Psalm 107:19-20** says, *"Then they cried to the Lord in their trouble, and he saved them from their distress. He sent out his word and healed them; he rescued them from the grave."* Meditating on such verses can deepen your connection to God's healing power.

Prayer for Strength and Vitality

Good health isn't just about being free from illness; it's also about having the strength and vitality to enjoy life and fulfill our purpose. We need energy to carry out our daily tasks, care for our loved ones, and pursue our goals. When our strength wanes, whether due to fatigue, stress, or other factors, it's essential to turn to God for renewal.

Heavenly Father,

I ask for Your strength today. My body feels tired, and my energy is low. I need Your help to restore my vitality. Fill me with Your divine energy so that I may face the day with renewed strength and purpose. Help me to remember that You are the source of all life and that I can draw upon Your endless supply of power. Guide me to make choices that support my physical health, and give me the discipline to rest and recharge when needed. Thank You for the gift of life and for the strength You provide to live it fully.

Amen.

This prayer focuses on the importance of strength and vitality in daily life. It's a request for God to infuse us with the energy we need to navigate our responsibilities and enjoy life's blessings. Strength can be both physical and spiritual, and this prayer acknowledges that true vitality comes from a deep connection with the Divine.

In the Bible, **Isaiah 40:31** offers encouragement: "*But those who hope in the Lord will renew their strength. They will soar on wings like eagles; they will run and not grow weary, they will walk and not be faint.*" Reflecting on this verse can remind us that God's strength is always available to us, even in our weakest moments.

Prayer for Protection from Sickness

In a world where illness and disease are constant threats, it's natural to seek God's protection. Whether we are concerned about a specific illness or simply want to safeguard our health, prayer can be a powerful way to ask for divine protection and peace of mind.

Lord of All Creation,
I ask for Your protection over my health. Shield me from

sickness and disease, and keep my body strong and resilient. In a world filled with uncertainties, I place my trust in Your unfailing love and care. Surround me with Your angels, that they may guard me from all harm. Guide me in making healthy choices that honor the body You have given me. Should illness come, grant me the wisdom to seek the right care and the strength to endure. But above all, help me to rest in the assurance that You are with me, no matter what challenges may arise.

Amen.

This prayer is an appeal for God's protective power over our health. It recognizes that while we can do our best to stay healthy, ultimately, we rely on God's protection. This prayer also encourages us to be proactive in caring for our bodies while trusting in God's overarching plan.

A comforting scripture for this prayer is **Psalm 91:10–11**: *"No harm will overtake you, no disaster will come near your tent. For he will command his angels concerning you to guard you in all your ways."* Reflecting on this verse can bring peace and confidence in God's protective presence.

Prayer for a Healthy Body

Maintaining a healthy body is essential for living a fulfilling and productive life. It requires a balance of proper nutrition, regular exercise, adequate rest, and a positive mindset. In this prayer, we ask God to help us care for our bodies and bless us with good health.

Gracious God,

Thank You for the gift of my body, a wondrous creation made in Your image. I pray for Your guidance in maintaining a healthy body. Help me to make wise choices in what I eat, how I exercise, and how I rest. Give me the discipline to care for this body as a temple of Your spirit. I ask for Your blessing on my physical health, that I may have the strength and vitality to serve You and others. Keep me free from harm, and help me to avoid habits that could damage my health. Thank You for the miracle of life and for the opportunity to live it in good health.

Amen.

This prayer emphasizes the importance of self-care and acknowledges that our bodies are sacred gifts from God. It's a reminder that taking care of our physical health is a way of honoring the Creator. This prayer also asks for God's help in making healthy choices and avoiding behaviors that could harm our bodies.

1 Corinthians 6:19-20 reminds us of the sacredness of our bodies: "*Do you not know that your bodies are temples of the Holy Spirit, who is in you, whom you have received from God? You are not your own; you were bought at a price. Therefore honor God with your bodies.*" This verse can inspire us to see our bodies as holy and to care for them with reverence.

Prayer for Restful Sleep and Recovery

Rest is a fundamental component of good health. Our bodies and minds need regular, restorative sleep to function optimally. Yet, in a world filled with stress and distractions, restful sleep can be elusive. This prayer asks God to grant us the peaceful rest we need to recover and rejuvenate.

Loving Father,

I come to You at the end of this day, seeking Your gift of restful sleep. My body and mind are weary, and I long for the peace that only You can provide. Please calm my thoughts and soothe my soul, that I may drift into a deep, restorative sleep. Remove any anxieties or worries that may disturb my rest. I ask for Your protection during the night, that I may wake up refreshed and ready to face a new day. Thank You for the gift of sleep, and for the renewal it brings. May I rest in Your arms, secure in Your love and care.

Amen.

This prayer highlights the importance of sleep as a time for the body and mind to recover from the day's activities. It's a request for peaceful, undisturbed sleep, and for God's protection throughout the night. Sleep is not only necessary for physical health but also for mental and emotional well-being.

Psalm 4:8 is a beautiful scripture to meditate on before sleep: *"In peace I will lie down and sleep, for you alone, Lord, make me dwell in safety."* This verse reassures us of God's watchful presence, allowing us to release our fears and rest peacefully.

PRAYERS FOR EMOTIONAL HEALTH

Prayer for Mental Clarity

In today's fast-paced world, our minds are often over-loaded with information, distractions, and worries. Mental clarity is essential for making sound decisions, maintaining focus, and living a purposeful life. When our thoughts are scattered, it can be challenging to find direction and peace. This prayer seeks God's guidance in clearing the mental fog and restoring clarity to our thoughts.

Heavenly Father,
I come before You with a mind that feels cluttered and over-whelmed. My thoughts are scattered, and I struggle to find clarity. Please help me to quiet my mind and focus on what truly matters. Grant me the wisdom to discern Your will for my life and the ability to see things clearly. Remove the confusion and distractions that cloud my judgment, and replace them with Your divine understanding. As I seek clarity, guide my thoughts toward truth and wisdom, and help me to make decisions that

honor You. Thank You for being the light that guides me through the fog of uncertainty.

Amen.

This prayer for mental clarity is a request for divine intervention in clearing the mind of confusion and distraction. It acknowledges the need for God's guidance in navigating life's complexities and making decisions that align with His will. Mental clarity is not just about thinking clearly; it's also about aligning our thoughts with God's truth and purpose.

In the Bible, **James 1:5** offers encouragement for those seeking wisdom: *"If any of you lacks wisdom, you should ask God, who gives generously to all without finding fault, and it will be given to you."* This verse reassures us that God is willing to provide the clarity and wisdom we need when we ask for it in faith.

Prayer for Overcoming Anxiety

Anxiety is a common struggle in our modern world, often fueled by stress, uncertainty, and fear of the unknown. It can feel like a heavy burden, weighing down the heart and mind. In times of anxiety, turning to prayer can provide relief and comfort, reminding us that we are not alone in our struggles and that God is always there to calm our fears.

Dear Lord,

My heart is heavy with anxiety, and my mind is troubled by worries. I feel overwhelmed by the challenges before me and uncertain about what the future holds. I ask for Your peace, the peace that surpasses all understanding, to fill my heart and calm my fears. Help me to release my anxieties to You, trusting that You are in control of all things. Give me the strength to face each day with courage and faith, knowing that You are with me every step of the way. Guide me to focus on Your promises and not on my fears, and let Your love cast out all anxiety.

Amen.

This prayer for overcoming anxiety is a heartfelt plea for God's peace and reassurance. It acknowledges the very real feelings of fear and worry that can overwhelm us, while also expressing trust in God's sovereignty and care. By surrendering our anxieties to God, we open ourselves to receiving His peace and strength.

Philippians 4:6-7 is a powerful scripture to meditate on when dealing with anxiety: "*Do not be anxious about anything, but in every situation, by prayer and petition, with thanksgiving, present your requests to God. And the peace of God, which transcends all understanding, will guard your hearts and your minds in Christ Jesus.*" This verse encourages us to bring our anxieties to God in prayer, with the assurance that His peace will guard our hearts and minds.

Prayer for Emotional Balance

Life is full of ups and downs, and it can be challenging to maintain emotional balance in the face of changing circumstances.

Emotional balance is about finding stability and peace within ourselves, even when external situations are tumultuous. This prayer asks God to help us navigate our emotions with grace, wisdom, and a steady heart.

Gracious God,

I ask for Your help in maintaining emotional balance in my life. There are times when my emotions feel like a storm, tossing me from one extreme to another. Please give me the strength to remain steady and calm, even in the face of challenges. Help me to manage my emotions with wisdom and grace, and to respond to situations with a heart full of love and patience. Teach me to recognize when my emotions are getting the better of me, and guide me to seek Your peace in those moments. Thank You for being my anchor, the source of my stability in an ever-changing world.

Amen.

This prayer for emotional balance recognizes the challenges of navigating life's emotional highs and lows. It is a request for God's guidance in maintaining a steady heart and mind, regardless of external circumstances. Emotional balance is crucial for mental health and well-being, and this prayer seeks to cultivate that inner peace.

Proverbs 4:23 offers wisdom on guarding our hearts: *"Above all else, guard your heart, for everything you do flows from it."* This verse reminds us of the importance of emotional balance and the need to protect our hearts from the negative influences that can disrupt our peace.

Prayer for Healing from Trauma

Trauma can leave deep emotional scars, affecting our ability to trust, love, and find joy in life. Healing from trauma is a journey that requires time, patience, and the support of loved ones—and, above all, the healing power of God. This prayer seeks God's comfort and strength in the process of emotional healing, asking for His touch to mend the brokenness within.

Loving Father,

I come to You with a heart that has been wounded by trauma. The pain I carry feels overwhelming, and at times, I struggle to move forward. I ask for Your healing touch to mend the broken places in my heart. Please bring comfort to my soul and peace to my mind. Help me to release the pain, anger, and fear that have taken root in my life. Guide me on the path of healing, and surround me with Your love and grace. I trust that You can restore what has been lost and bring beauty from the ashes of my pain. Thank You for being my healer and my refuge in times of trouble.

Amen.

This prayer for healing from trauma is a deeply personal plea for God's comfort and restoration. It acknowledges the pain and suffering caused by trauma while expressing faith in God's ability to heal even the deepest wounds. Healing from trauma is a journey, and this prayer invites God to walk alongside us on that path.

Psalm 147:3 provides a comforting reminder of God's healing power: "*He heals the brokenhearted and binds up their wounds.*" This verse reassures us that God is close to those who are hurting and that He is capable of healing even the most profound emotional wounds.

Prayer for Peace of Mind

Peace of mind is a precious gift, especially in a world filled with chaos, noise, and constant demands. Achieving a state of inner peace requires letting go of worries, trusting in God, and focusing on His presence in our lives. This prayer seeks God's peace to calm our minds, helping us to find tranquility amidst life's challenges.

Lord of Peace,

I long for peace of mind, a calm and tranquil heart that is not easily disturbed by the cares of this world. My mind is often filled with worries, fears, and endless thoughts that rob me of peace. Please quiet my mind and bring Your peace into my heart. Help me to let go of the things I cannot control and to trust in Your plan for my life. Teach me to dwell in Your presence, where true peace is found. May Your peace guard my mind and guide my thoughts, leading me to a place of rest and serenity. Thank You for being the source of all peace, a refuge in the midst of life's storms.

Amen.

This prayer for peace of mind is an appeal for God's calming presence to fill our hearts and minds. It recognizes the challenges of maintaining peace in a world full of distractions and stresses, and it seeks God's help in finding and holding onto that peace. Peace of mind is not just the absence of conflict but the presence of God's serenity within us.

Isaiah 26:3 is a powerful scripture that speaks to the promise of peace: *"You will keep in perfect peace those whose minds are steadfast, because they trust in you."* This verse encourages us to keep our minds focused on God, trusting in Him to provide the peace that surpasses all understanding.

PRAYERS FOR SPIRITUAL HEALTH

Prayer for Inner Peace

In our noisy, hectic world, finding inner peace can be a challenge. We are often pulled in many directions, overwhelmed by stress, and consumed by worry. Yet, true peace comes not from our external circumstances but from within, where we can connect with the divine presence of God. This prayer seeks to cultivate that deep sense of tranquility that only God can provide.

Dear God,

I come before You with a heart that is restless and a mind that is troubled by the cares of this world. I long for the peace that only You can give—the peace that surpasses all understanding. Help me to quiet my mind and calm my spirit so that I may rest in Your presence. Teach me to trust in Your divine plan for my life, knowing that You hold all things in Your hands. Fill me with Your peace, and let it flow through every part of my being, bringing calm to my soul. Guide me to release my worries and

fears to You, and help me to find solace in Your love.
Amen.

This prayer for inner peace focuses on releasing the burdens that weigh us down and finding refuge in God's presence. Inner peace is not about escaping life's challenges but rather about experiencing calm in the midst of them. By turning to God in prayer, we can access a deep sense of peace that transcends our circumstances.

Philippians 4:7 reassures us of the peace that comes from God: *"And the peace of God, which transcends all understanding, will guard your hearts and your minds in Christ Jesus."* Reflecting on this verse can help us trust that God's peace will protect us, even when the world around us is in turmoil.

Prayer for Strengthening Faith

Faith is the foundation of our spiritual life. It is through faith that we trust in God's promises, find hope in difficult times, and maintain our relationship with the Divine. However, there are times when our faith may waver—when doubts creep in, and our trust in God feels shaky. This prayer seeks to strengthen and renew our faith, helping us to stand firm in our beliefs.

Heavenly Father,
I come to You with a heart that desires to grow in faith. At times, my faith feels weak, and I struggle with doubt and uncertainty. Please strengthen my faith, so that I may trust in

You fully and without hesitation. Help me to see beyond my circumstances and to place my confidence in Your unchanging love and power. When I face trials and challenges, remind me of Your promises and the countless times You have been faithful in my life. Give me the courage to hold on to my faith, even when the road ahead is unclear. Thank You for being the rock upon which I can build my life.

Amen.

This prayer for strengthening faith acknowledges the difficulties we sometimes face in maintaining our trust in God. It's a request for God to fortify our faith, giving us the strength to believe even when we encounter doubts. Strong faith is essential for spiritual health, as it anchors us in God's truth and love.

Hebrews 11:1 provides a powerful definition of faith: *"Now faith is confidence in what we hope for and assurance about what we do not see."* Meditating on this verse can remind us that faith is about trusting in God's promises, even when we cannot see the outcome.

Prayer for Spiritual Renewal

There are times in our spiritual journey when we may feel distant from God, when our relationship with Him seems to have grown cold or stagnant. These are moments when we need spiritual renewal—a rekindling of our passion for God and a deepening of our connection with Him. This prayer seeks God's help in reviving our spiritual lives, bringing new energy and enthusiasm to our faith.

Gracious God,

I come to You seeking renewal in my spirit. There are times when I feel distant from You, when my heart is not as passionate as it once was. I ask for Your Holy Spirit to breathe new life into my soul. Rekindle the fire of my faith and draw me closer to You. Help me to remove anything in my life that is hindering my relationship with You, and fill me with a renewed sense of purpose and devotion. May my heart overflow with love for You, and may my life reflect the joy of walking in Your light. Thank You for Your grace and mercy, which are new every morning.

Amen.

This prayer for spiritual renewal is a plea for God to revive our spiritual lives and restore our passion for Him. It acknowledges the times when we may feel spiritually dry and asks for a fresh outpouring of God's Spirit to renew our hearts. Spiritual renewal is essential for maintaining a vibrant and dynamic relationship with God.

Psalm 51:10 is a beautiful scripture to accompany this prayer: *"Create in me a pure heart, O God, and renew a steadfast spirit within me."* This verse captures the essence of spiritual renewal— asking God to cleanse our hearts and restore our commitment to Him.

Prayer for Joy and Contentment

Joy and contentment are fruits of a healthy spiritual life. They are not dependent on our external circumstances but are rooted in our relationship with God. When we are spiritually healthy, we can experience joy and contentment even in the midst of challenges. This prayer asks God to fill our hearts with joy and contentment, helping us to find satisfaction and happiness in Him.

Loving Father,

I thank You for the many blessings You have given me, and I ask for Your help in cultivating joy and contentment in my life. Help me to find joy not in the fleeting pleasures of this world but in the enduring relationship I have with You. Teach me to be content with what I have, trusting that You provide for all my needs. When I am tempted to compare myself to others or to seek fulfillment in material things, remind me that true joy and contentment are found in You alone. Fill my heart with gratitude and peace, and let my life be a reflection of Your goodness.

Amen.

This prayer for joy and contentment focuses on finding true happiness and satisfaction in God, rather than in external circumstances. It's a reminder that joy and contentment are spiritual gifts that come from a deep and abiding relationship with God. By focusing on gratitude and trust in God's provision, we can experience lasting joy and peace.

Philippians 4:11-13 offers a powerful lesson in contentment:

"I am not saying this because I am in need, for I have learned to be content whatever the circumstances. I know what it is to be in need, and I know what it is to have plenty. I have learned the secret of being content in any and every situation, whether well fed or hungry, whether living in plenty or in want. I can do all this through him who gives me strength." This passage encourages us to find contentment in all circumstances, relying on God's strength to sustain us.

Prayer for a Healthy Spirit

Our spiritual health is the foundation of our overall well-being. A healthy spirit is one that is connected to God, rooted in His Word, and guided by His Spirit. It is through our spiritual health that we find purpose, meaning, and direction in life. This prayer asks God to nurture and strengthen our spirit, helping us to grow in faith and live according to His will.

Holy God,

I thank You for the gift of life and for the spirit You have placed within me. I ask that You help me to cultivate a healthy spirit, one that is strong in faith, rich in love, and grounded in Your truth. Guide me to spend time in Your Word and in prayer, so that I may grow closer to You each day. Help me to listen to the promptings of Your Holy Spirit and to follow Your guidance in all that I do. Keep my spirit pure and free from anything that would separate me from You. May my life be a reflection of Your love, grace, and truth.

Amen.

This prayer for a healthy spirit is a request for God's help in nurturing our spiritual well-being. It emphasizes the importance of staying connected to God through prayer, scripture, and obedience to His will. A healthy spirit is one that is aligned with God's purpose and filled with His love.

Galatians 5:22-23 describes the fruits of a healthy spirit: "*But the fruit of the Spirit is love, joy, peace, forbearance, kindness, goodness, faithfulness, gentleness and self-control. Against such things there is no law.*" This passage reminds us of the qualities that characterize a healthy, Spirit-filled life.

PRAYERS FOR LOVED ONES' HEALTH

Prayer for the Health of a Child

Children are precious gifts from God, and as parents or guardians, we naturally worry about their health and well-being. Whether a child is dealing with illness or we simply wish to pray for their continued health, turning to God in prayer is a powerful way to seek His protection and blessings for them. This prayer is a heartfelt plea for God's loving care over the health of a child.

Heavenly Father,

I thank You for the precious gift of this child. You have entrusted me with their care, and I am deeply grateful for the joy they bring into my life. I come to You today to ask for Your protection over their health. Keep them safe from illness and injury, and grant them strength and vitality as they grow. If they are facing any health challenges, I pray for Your healing touch to restore them to full health. Surround them with Your love and peace, and guide me as I care for their physical, emotional, and spiritual needs. Thank You for watching over them and for being their protector and healer.

Amen.

This prayer for the health of a child is a tender expression of love and concern, asking God to watch over and protect the child's well-being. It acknowledges the deep responsibility and love that comes with caring for a child and places that child's health in God's capable hands.

Psalm 127:3 reminds us of the blessing that children are: "*Children are a heritage from the Lord, offspring a reward from him.*" This verse can inspire us to approach the care of children with gratitude and reverence, trusting in God's provision for their health and growth.

Prayer for a Spouse's Health

Our spouses are our closest companions in life, sharing in both our joys and our challenges. When they face health issues, it can be a source of deep concern and anxiety. Praying for a spouse's health is an act of love and faith, asking God to sustain and heal them so that they may continue to thrive in their life together. This prayer seeks God's intervention and care for the health of a spouse.

Loving God,

I thank You for the gift of my spouse, who is my partner in life and my closest friend. I lift them up to You now, asking for Your healing power and protection over their health. Please bless them with strength and vitality, and keep them free from illness and harm. If they are currently struggling with health issues, I pray for Your healing touch to bring them relief and restoration. Give me the wisdom and patience to support them during this time, and help us to draw closer to each other and to You through this experience. Thank You for being our refuge and strength, a very present help in times of trouble.

Amen.

This prayer for a spouse's health expresses deep love and concern, seeking God's care and healing for a beloved partner. It also acknowledges the shared journey of marriage, where spouses support and care for each other, especially in times of need.

Ephesians 5:28-29 provides a beautiful perspective on the love and care spouses should have for one another: "*In this same way, husbands ought to love their wives as their own bodies. He who loves his wife loves himself. After all, no one ever hated their own body, but they feed and care for their body, just as Christ does the church.*" This passage emphasizes the importance of nurturing and caring for one's spouse, reflecting the love that Christ has for His people.

Prayer for Elderly Parents

As our parents age, they may face a variety of health challenges. Watching our parents grow older and struggle with their health can be difficult, but it is also an opportunity to care for them as they have cared for us. Praying for the health of elderly parents is a way to honor them and to seek God's comfort and strength for them in their later years.

Dear Lord,

I thank You for the blessing of my parents, who have given me life and have cared for me throughout the years. As they grow older, I ask for Your special care over their health. Please protect them from illness and grant them the strength they need to enjoy their remaining years. If they are dealing with health challenges, I pray for Your healing touch and for peace in their hearts. Help me to be a source of comfort and support for them, and give me the wisdom to assist them in whatever ways they need. Thank You for the love and care they have given me, and for the opportunity to care for them in return.

Amen.

This prayer for elderly parents is a touching expression of gratitude and concern, asking God to watch over the health of those who have given so much to us. It recognizes the natural process of aging and seeks God's comfort and care for parents in their later years.

Isaiah 46:4 offers a reassuring promise for the elderly: "*Even to your old age and gray hairs I am he, I am he who will sustain you. I have made you and I will carry you; I will sustain you and I will rescue you.*" This verse can bring comfort to both elderly parents and their children, reminding them of God's enduring care throughout all stages of life.

Prayer for a Friend's Healing

When a friend is going through a health crisis, it can be a challenging time for both them and those who care about them. Offering prayers for a friend's healing is a way to support them spiritually, showing that we care deeply for their well-being. This prayer asks God to bring healing and comfort to a dear friend in need.

Compassionate God,

I lift up my dear friend to You, who is in need of Your healing touch. You know the struggles they are facing, and I ask that You bring them comfort and relief. Please guide the hands of the doctors and caregivers, and grant them the wisdom they need to provide the best care possible. I pray for strength and peace for my friend, that they may feel Your presence with them through this difficult time. Help me to be a source of encouragement and support, and give me the right words to say to bring comfort to their heart. Thank You for the gift of friendship and for being our ultimate healer.

Amen.

This prayer for a friend's healing is a heartfelt request for God's intervention and comfort during a difficult time. It expresses the love and concern we have for our friends, as well as our trust in God's power to heal and restore.

James 5:16 encourages us to pray for one another: "*Therefore confess your sins to each other and pray for each other so that you may be healed. The prayer of a righteous person is powerful* *and effective.*" This verse reminds us of the importance of intercessory prayer, especially in times of illness.

Prayer for Community Well-Being

Our communities are an integral part of our lives, providing us with connection, support, and a sense of belonging. The health of our community members affects us all, and praying for the well-being of our community is a way to seek God's blessings for the collective good. This prayer asks for God's protection, health, and unity within our community.

Lord of All,

I pray for the well-being of my community, the people who surround me and share in this journey of life. I ask for Your protection over each person, that they may be kept safe from illness and harm. Please bring healing to those who are suffering, and grant strength to those who are caring for others. Help us to support one another, to show kindness and compassion, and to work together for the common good. May our community be a place of peace, health, and unity, where Your love is evident in all that we do. Thank You for the blessings of community, and for the opportunity to make a positive difference in the lives of others.

Amen.

This prayer for community well-being reflects the interconnectedness of our lives and the importance of supporting each other's health and happiness. It is a request for God's blessings on the community as a whole, seeking unity and collective well-being.

Romans 12:4-5 speaks to the importance of community: "*For just as each of us has one body with many members, and these members do not all have the same function, so in Christ we, though many, form one body, and each member belongs to all the others.*" This passage reminds us that we are all part of a greater whole and that the health and well-being of one affects us all.

PRAYERS FOR HEALTHY HABITS

Prayer for Healthy Eating

Maintaining a healthy diet is crucial for physical well-being and overall health. However, in a world filled with fast food, processed snacks, and busy schedules, it can be challenging to make wise food choices consistently. Healthy eating is about more than just nourishing our bodies—it's also about honoring God's creation by taking care of the bodies He has given us. This prayer seeks God's guidance in cultivating mindful eating habits that contribute to our health and vitality.

Heavenly Father,

I thank You for the abundance of food that You provide, and for the nourishment it brings to my body. I ask for Your help in making healthy choices when it comes to my diet. Guide me to eat foods that are wholesome and nutritious, and give me the discipline to avoid those that harm my health. Help me to be mindful of what I put into my body, recognizing it as a temple of

Your Holy Spirit. Teach me to eat in moderation, with gratitude for the blessings of each meal. May my eating habits honor You and contribute to my overall well-being, so that I may serve You with strength and energy.

Amen.

This prayer for healthy eating focuses on the importance of making mindful, nutritious choices that support our physical health and align with our spiritual values. It acknowledges the challenges of maintaining a healthy diet in today's world and asks for God's guidance in cultivating habits that honor our bodies as temples of the Holy Spirit.

1 Corinthians 10:31 reminds us of the spiritual significance of our daily actions: *"So whether you eat or drink or whatever you do, do it all for the glory of God."* Reflecting on this verse can inspire us to approach our eating habits with a sense of reverence and gratitude, making choices that honor God.

Prayer for Consistent Exercise

Physical activity is essential for maintaining good health, improving mood, and enhancing overall well-being. Yet, finding the motivation and time to exercise regularly can be difficult. Consistent exercise requires discipline, commitment, and a positive mindset. This prayer seeks God's help in developing a regular exercise routine that supports our physical health and honors the bodies He has given us.

Dear Lord,

I ask for Your guidance in making physical activity a regular part of my life. You have created my body with the ability to move, and I want to use this gift to its fullest. Help me to find joy in exercise, whether it's walking, running, dancing, or any other activity that keeps me healthy and strong. Give me the motivation to stick with a consistent exercise routine, even on days when I feel tired or unmotivated. Let my physical activity be a way to honor You, by taking care of the body You have entrusted to me. Thank You for the strength and energy You provide, and for the opportunity to live an active, healthy life.

Amen.

This prayer for consistent exercise highlights the importance of physical activity in maintaining health and well-being. It acknowledges the challenges of staying motivated and asks for God's help in establishing a regular exercise routine that brings joy and honors His creation.

1 Timothy 4:8 offers a balanced perspective on physical exercise: *"For physical training is of some value, but godliness has value for all things, holding promise for both the present life and the life to come."* This verse reminds us that while physical exercise is important, it should be balanced with spiritual growth and devotion.

Prayer for Breaking Unhealthy Habits

We all have habits that may not serve our best interests— whether it's overeating, smoking, excessive screen time, or any other behavior that negatively impacts our health. Breaking unhealthy habits can be challenging, but with God's help, it is possible to overcome them and replace them with habits that promote our well-being. This prayer seeks God's strength and guidance in breaking free from habits that hinder our health and spiritual growth.

Gracious God,

I come to You with a humble heart, recognizing that there are habits in my life that do not honor You or contribute to my well-being. I ask for Your help in breaking these unhealthy patterns and replacing them with habits that support my health and spiritual growth. Give me the strength to resist temptation and the wisdom to make choices that align with Your will for my life. Surround me with supportive people who will encourage me on this journey, and help me to be patient and persistent as I work to overcome these habits. Thank You for Your grace and for the new beginnings You offer each day.

Amen.

This prayer for breaking unhealthy habits acknowledges the difficulty of changing long-established patterns but also expresses hope and trust in God's ability to help us overcome them. It emphasizes the importance of relying on God's strength and guidance in making lasting changes that improve our health and well-being.

Romans 12:2 provides inspiration for transformation: *"Do not conform to the pattern of this world, but be transformed by the renewing of your mind. Then you will be able to test and approve what God's will is—his good, pleasing and perfect will."* This verse encourages us to seek transformation through God's guidance, breaking free from unhealthy patterns and aligning our lives with His will.

Prayer for Self-Care and Rest

In our busy lives, it's easy to neglect self-care and rest. However, taking time to care for ourselves is essential for maintaining our health, preventing burnout, and staying connected with God. Rest is not only a physical need but also a spiritual practice, allowing us to recharge and reflect on God's presence in our lives. This prayer asks God to help us prioritize self-care and rest, recognizing their importance in our overall well-being.

Loving Father,

I thank You for the gift of rest and the opportunity to care for the body, mind, and spirit that You have given me. Help me to prioritize self-care in my life, recognizing that I cannot pour from an empty cup. Guide me to find balance between work and rest, and to take time each day to recharge and reconnect with You. When I am tempted to overextend myself, remind me of the importance of rest and the example of Sabbath You have set before me. May my times of rest be a source of renewal and peace, allowing me to serve You with a refreshed and joyful heart.

Amen.

This prayer for self-care and rest emphasizes the importance of taking time to recharge, both physically and spiritually. It acknowledges the temptation to neglect self-care in the pursuit of productivity and asks for God's guidance in finding balance and prioritizing rest.

Exodus 20:8-10 reminds us of the importance of Sabbath rest: *"Remember the Sabbath day by keeping it holy. Six days you shall labor and do all your work, but the seventh day is a sabbath to the Lord your God. On it you shall not do any work, neither you, nor your son or daughter, nor your male or female servant, nor your animals, nor any foreigner residing in your towns."* This commandment highlights the significance of rest as a time to focus on God and recharge our spirits.

Prayer for Healthy Living

Healthy living encompasses all aspects of our well-being—physical, emotional, and spiritual. It's about making choices that support a balanced and fulfilling life, grounded in our relationship with God. This prayer seeks God's help in living a life that reflects His love and care, promoting health and wholeness in every area of our lives.

Lord of Life,

I thank You for the gift of life and for the many blessings You have bestowed upon me. I ask for Your guidance in living a life that is healthy and balanced, honoring You in all that I do. Help me to make choices that support my physical health, such as eating well, exercising, and getting enough rest. Guide me to cultivate positive relationships and to nurture my emotional well-being. Above all, help me to grow in my spiritual life, deepening my connection with You each day. May my life be a reflection of Your love, grace, and truth, and may I inspire others to pursue health and wholeness in their own lives.

Amen.

This prayer for healthy living is a comprehensive request for God's guidance in all aspects of our well-being. It emphasizes the interconnectedness of physical, emotional, and spiritual health and asks for God's help in making choices that promote a balanced and fulfilling life.

3 John 1:2 expresses a prayer for holistic well-being: *"Dear friend, I pray that you may enjoy good health and that all may go well with you, even as your soul is getting along well."* This verse reflects the desire for overall health and prosperity, both physically and spiritually.

PRAYERS OF GRATITUDE FOR HEALTH

Prayer of Thanks for Healing

Healing, whether physical, emotional, or spiritual, is a profound blessing that reflects God's love and power. When we experience healing, it's important to pause and offer thanks to God for His mercy and care. This prayer is an expression of deep gratitude for the healing that has taken place in our lives, acknowledging God as the source of all health and wholeness.

Heavenly Father,

I come before You with a heart full of gratitude for the healing You have brought into my life. There were times when I felt weak and uncertain, but You were always there, guiding me through the pain and bringing me to a place of health and peace. Thank You for Your healing touch, for restoring my body, mind, and spirit. I recognize that all healing comes from You, and I am deeply thankful for Your mercy and grace. Help me to use this gift of renewed health to serve You better and to share Your love with others. May I never take this blessing for granted, but always remember to give thanks to You, my Great Physician.

Amen.

This prayer of thanks for healing focuses on acknowledging God's role in the healing process and expressing gratitude for the restoration of health. It encourages a spirit of thankfulness and reminds us to use our renewed strength in service to God and others.

Psalm 103:2-3 serves as a beautiful reminder of God's healing power: *"Praise the Lord, my soul, and forget not all his benefits—who forgives all your sins and heals all your diseases."* This passage encourages us to remember and be grateful for God's continuous acts of healing and forgiveness.

Prayer of Gratitude for Daily Health

The simple gift of good health is something many of us may take for granted as we go about our daily lives. However, being healthy allows us to work, care for our loved ones, and enjoy life's many blessings. This prayer is an expression of gratitude for the everyday health that enables us to live fully and with purpose.

Gracious God,

Thank You for the gift of health that You provide each day. I am grateful for the strength and energy that allow me to carry out my daily tasks and to enjoy the many blessings in my life. Help me to never take this gift for granted, but to appreciate each moment of good health. I recognize that every breath I take, every step I walk, and every task I accomplish is possible because of Your sustaining grace. Please continue to bless me with health, and guide me in making choices that honor this gift. May I always be mindful of Your goodness, giving thanks to You in all things.

Amen.

This prayer of gratitude for daily health is a reminder to appreciate the often-overlooked blessing of simply being healthy. It encourages us to recognize God's role in sustaining our well-being and to live with a constant awareness of His provision.

3 John 1:2 expresses a similar sentiment: *"Dear friend, I pray that you may enjoy good health and that all may go well with you, even as your soul is getting along well."* This verse reflects the wish for continued health and well-being, acknowledging the importance of both physical and spiritual health.

Prayer for the Health of Family and Friends

The health and well-being of our loved ones are deeply important to us. When our family and friends are healthy, it brings us great joy and peace. This prayer is an expression of gratitude for the health of those we care about, recognizing God's protection and provision over their lives.

Loving Father,

I thank You for the health and well-being of my family and friends. It is a great comfort to know that they are safe, healthy, and thriving. I am grateful for Your protection over them, and for the many ways You care for their physical, emotional, and spiritual needs. Please continue to watch over them, keeping them free from illness and harm. Help us to support each other in living healthy lives, and to always be there for one another in times of need. I praise You for the gift of these relationships and for the joy that comes from sharing life with those I love.

Amen.

This prayer for the health of family and friends emphasizes the joy and gratitude we feel when our loved ones are in good health. It also acknowledges the importance of God's protection and care in their lives.

Psalm 121:7-8 offers reassurance of God's protection: *"The Lord will keep you from all harm—he will watch over your life; the Lord will watch over your coming and going both now and forevermore."* This passage reminds us that God's care extends to every aspect of our loved ones' lives, providing peace of mind and gratitude.

Prayer of Appreciation for Medical Care

In times of illness or injury, we are often blessed with the care and expertise of medical professionals who work tirelessly to help us heal. This prayer is an expression of gratitude for the doctors, nurses, and other healthcare providers who dedicate their lives to caring for others. It also acknowledges the role that medical care plays in the healing process, alongside God's divine intervention.

Dear Lord,

I thank You for the blessing of medical care and for the skilled professionals who dedicate their lives to helping others. I am grateful for the doctors, nurses, and all healthcare workers who have cared for me and my loved ones with compassion and expertise. Thank You for the knowledge and wisdom You have given them, and for the advancements in medicine that have made healing possible. Please bless those who work in the medical field, giving them strength, wisdom, and protection as they continue to serve others. I recognize that while they provide the care, all healing ultimately comes from You, and I am deeply thankful for Your guidance in their work.

Amen.

This prayer of appreciation for medical care acknowledges the important role that healthcare professionals play in our healing journeys. It expresses gratitude for their dedication and skill while recognizing that God is the ultimate source of all healing.

Sirach 38:1-2 (from the Apocrypha) offers a fitting reflection: *"Honor the physician with the honor due him, according to your need of him, for the Lord created him; for healing comes from the Most High, and he will receive a gift from the king."* This passage highlights the importance of honoring those who provide medical care, acknowledging their role as instruments of God's healing.

Prayer of Thanksgiving for God's Protection

Throughout our lives, we often encounter situations that could potentially harm our health—whether it's accidents, illnesses, or other dangers. Yet, many times, we find ourselves protected and unharmed, often without realizing it. This prayer is a heart-felt expression of gratitude for God's continuous protection over our health and safety, recognizing His hand in keeping us safe from harm.

Almighty God,

I thank You for the countless times You have protected me from harm, often in ways I may not even realize. Your hand has been upon me, shielding me from accidents, illness, and danger, and I am deeply grateful for Your care. I recognize that it is because of Your protection that I am here today, healthy and safe. Please continue to watch over me and my loved ones, guiding us away from harm and keeping us in Your loving care. Help me to always trust in Your protection, knowing that You are with me in every situation. I give thanks to You for Your unfailing love and for the peace that comes from knowing I am in Your hands.

Amen.

This prayer of thanksgiving for God's protection reflects a deep awareness of God's constant care and the many ways He keeps us safe, often without our knowledge. It is a reminder to be grateful for His ongoing presence and protection in our lives.

Psalm 91:4 offers a powerful image of God's protective care:

"He will cover you with his feathers, and under his wings you will find refuge; his faithfulness will be your shield and rampart." This verse provides a comforting reminder of God's protective embrace, shielding us from harm and providing a place of safety.

CONCLUSION

As you reach the end of this prayer book, I hope that you feel a renewed sense of peace, strength, and connection to God. The prayers within these pages are meant to guide you on your journey toward good health, providing comfort, encouragement, and spiritual support at every step of the way. Whether you have been seeking physical healing, emotional balance, or spiritual renewal, these prayers are tools to help you draw closer to God and to experience the wholeness He desires for you.

Reflecting on the Gift of Health

Health is one of the greatest gifts we can receive, yet it is also one of the most fragile. Throughout this book, we have explored the many dimensions of health—physical, emotional, and spiritual—and how each of these aspects is interconnected. True health is not just the absence of illness but a state of overall well-being that encompasses body, mind, and spirit.

As you reflect on the prayers and insights shared in this book, take a moment to appreciate the gift of health in your own life. Consider the times when you have been blessed with good health and the moments when you have experienced healing. Think about the ways in which God has sustained you through challenges and how He has provided for your needs. It is through these reflections that we come to understand the depth of God's love and care for us.

The journey to good health is ongoing, and it is one that requires constant attention and care. By incorporating prayer into your daily routine, you are inviting God to be an active participant in your health journey. You are acknowledging that true health comes from Him and that by aligning your life with His will, you can experience the fullness of His blessings.

Continuing the Practice of Prayer

One of the key messages of this book is the importance of prayer in maintaining good health. Prayer is a powerful tool that allows us to connect with God, express our deepest desires, and seek His guidance and support. As you move forward, I encourage you to continue the practice of prayer, making it an integral part of your daily life.

Here are some practical ways to continue the practice of prayer as you pursue good health:

Daily Prayer: Set aside a specific time each day to pray for your health and the health of your loved ones. This could be in the morning to start your day with strength and clarity, or in the evening to reflect on the day and seek rest and renewal.

Scripture Meditation: Choose a Bible verse that resonates with your current health journey and meditate on it throughout the day. Let the words of Scripture guide your thoughts and actions, bringing you closer to God's will for your life.

Gratitude Journal: Keep a journal where you write down your prayers of gratitude for the health you have and the healing you have received. Reflecting on these blessings will help you maintain a positive outlook and a heart full of thankfulness.

Praying for Others: Extend your prayers to include those around you who may be struggling with their health. By praying for others, you are not only offering them support but also strengthening your own connection to God and the community.

Prayer Walks: Take time to go on a prayer walk, where you can enjoy the beauty of God's creation while offering prayers for your health and well-being. Walking can be both a physical exercise and a spiritual practice, helping you to integrate body, mind, and spirit.

Trusting in God's Plan

As you continue on your health journey, remember that there will be times of difficulty and uncertainty. Health challenges can arise unexpectedly, and they can test our faith and resilience. In these moments, it is important to trust in God's plan for your life, knowing that He is with you every step of the way.

Trusting in God's plan does not mean that you will always understand why certain things happen or that you will never experience pain or struggle. Rather, it means that you have faith in God's wisdom and love, believing that He is working all things for your good, even when the path ahead seems unclear.

When you face health challenges, use prayer as a way to seek comfort and guidance. Ask God to give you the strength to endure, the wisdom to make good decisions, and the peace to accept whatever comes your way. Remember that God is not distant or uninvolved; He is intimately aware of your needs and desires to walk with you through every trial.

Living a Life of Health and Wholeness

The ultimate goal of this prayer book is to help you live a life of health and wholeness—one that is rooted in a deep and abiding relationship with God. Health is not just about the physical body; it is about living in harmony with God's will and experiencing the fullness of life that He offers.

As you pursue good health, consider the following principles to guide your journey:

Balance: Strive for balance in all areas of your life—physical, emotional, and spiritual. Recognize that each aspect of your health is interconnected, and that true well-being comes from nurturing all parts of your being.

Mindfulness: Be mindful of the choices you make each day, whether it's the food you eat, the thoughts you entertain, or the activities you engage in. Choose habits that support your health and align with God's purpose for your life.

Gratitude: Cultivate a spirit of gratitude for the health you have, and for the many ways God blesses you each day. Gratitude has the power to transform your outlook and bring you closer to God's presence.

Service: Use your health and strength to serve others, whether through acts of kindness, volunteer work, or simply being there for those in need. By serving others, you are reflecting God's love and fulfilling His call to love your neighbor as yourself.

Faith: Keep your faith at the center of your health journey. Trust in God's provision, seek His guidance in all things, and remember that your health is a gift to be used for His glory.

A Final Word of Encouragement

As you close this book, I want to leave you with a final word of encouragement. No matter where you are on your health journey—whether you are in a season of strength or a time of struggle—know that God is with you. He is your healer, your protector, and your source of life. Turn to Him in prayer, and trust that He will provide for your every need.

Remember that your health is a precious gift, one that is meant to be cherished and nurtured. Take the lessons you have learned from this book and apply them to your daily life. Make prayer a regular practice, seek balance in all things, and live with a heart full of gratitude.

May you continue to grow in health, strength, and faith, and may you experience the fullness of God's blessings in your life. As you walk this journey of health and prayer, know that you are never alone—God is always with you, guiding you toward a life of wholeness and peace.

Amen.